Pray and Learn Numbers with Edgar G. Frog in the Valley of Numbers

Written and Illustrated By - Linda D. Washington
Edited By - Rita K. Jeffries

A PRAYER FOR THE CHILDREN

Father,

We ask that You put into each child's heart the desire to obey You and their parents in the Lord. Please give each of your children a heart to show love, to forgive and boldness to tell others about You and Jesus. Help us to listen and learn from You, Jesus and Holy Spirit. Thank You Father! In Jesus name we pray.

Amen

Dedicated to:
Micayah!
And to all children worldwide
in the hope that they choose to always pray, trust God our Father, Holy Spirit, and tell others about God's Son, Jesus Christ!

Story Introduction

Edgar G is four years old. Every day his parents prayed for him. Edgar G also liked to pray and talk with God, our Father in heaven. He learned that God the Father, His Son Jesus, and Holy Spirit would always help him when he prayed and asked. But sometimes Edgar G would forget to pray.

When Edgar G went to school he did not always listen when his teacher told him about numbers and how to count. Instead of asking God to help him pay attention, Edgar G would daydream of far-away lands where he could just hop and play all day. One day his wish suddenly happened. But it not only took him to a strange dream land, he also was changed into A FROG! Edgar G needs help.

Come join Edgar G Frog as he begins his next adventure in the
VALLEY OF NUMBERS

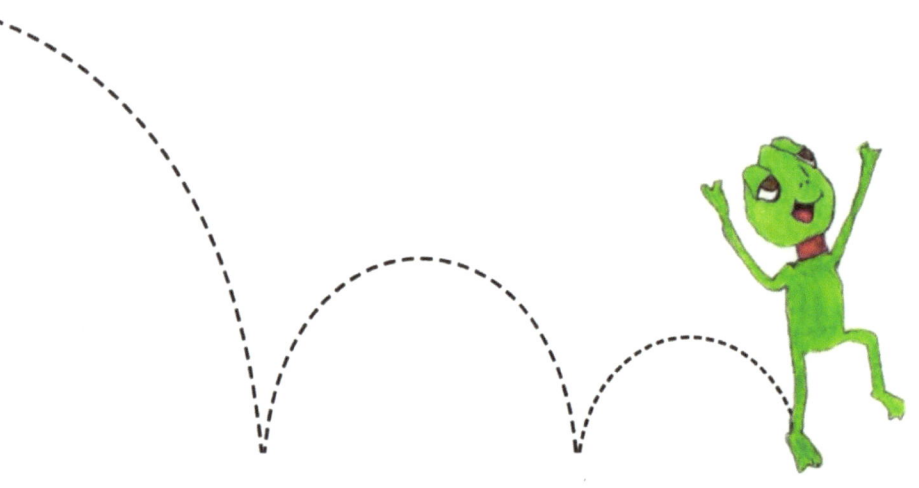

Edgar G Frog could hop FAST.

He hopped so fast and so far, that when he stopped, he was at the top of a big steep hill.

Edgar G looked around.
Then he saw it.
It was the biggest and deepest hole he had ever seen.
It was a valley!
The hill and the valley were covered with rocks.

Edgar G picked up a rock.

Just as he arched his arm to throw the rock deep into the valley, he remembered what his parents and teacher told him about safety.

They said, "Edgar you must play safely."

Edgar G thought, "My parents aren't here. I can do what I want to do."

He wound up his arm 1, 2, 3 times. He threw that big rock as far and his little green arm could throw.

THUMP! K E R - P L O P!

"O U C H!" Someone yelled from the valley.

"H-E-Y!" yelled Edgar G **"Who's that?"**

"Who's that?" someone yelled back at Edgar G. Surprised, Edgar G ran behind a nearby bush.

Edgar G shouted at the top of his voice, "WHO'S THAT SAYING WHO'S THAT?"

"It's me! It's Oink C, the voice snorted back.

Edgar G peeped into the valley.

Lying on the ground was a great big floppy hat *AND* beside the hat was ...
...A PIG!

Mr. Oink C Pig was picking himself up from the dirt, and Edgar G *knew* that it was his fault.

"Oops...Oh my!" Edgar G said.

Edgar G felt sad.

Tears came into his eyes as he said, **"I really didn't mean to hurt you. I was just doing what I wanted to do, so I...I, I threw a rock."**

"Sorry!" he said, as he dropped his frog head before asking, **"Are you all right?"**

"I'm fine. I'm fine!" snorted Oink as he brushed himself off and adjusted his large hat upon his head. "I was passing by when something whizzed past my face and blew my hat off my head. I lost my balance and fell to the ground."

"Don't you know it's dangerous to throw rocks little frog? "grunted Oink C Pig.

"I . . .uh... well . . . yes, I knew," Edgar G stuttered. "Actually, my parents taught me that I cannot always do what I feel like doing, especially if it hurts someone. They told me to choose to BE SAFE and to ALWAYS PRAY!"

"I should have obeyed my parents."

"*But* I can choose to obey them now and pray to my heavenly Father. *And* I know that Jesus will help me!"

"I'm sorry."
"Will you forgive me for throwing that rock?"

"Sure, little frog! I forgive you.
And my name is Oink C Pig."

"I'm really not a frog. My name is Edgar G.
I want to be what God made me to be, *a boy*.
But somehow here I am, a hopping green frog.
I'm on my way home,
if I can figure out which way to go."

"Well, Edgar G Frog," Oink snorted, **"you can either go forward or backwards."**

Edgar G looked back at the forest and shook his head.
"Oh no, I don't want to go backwards. I must go forward."

"Will you wait for me to come down there with you?"

"Sure I will!" said Oink.

"Is there a secret way to get through this valley?" Edgar G asked.

Oink said, "It's no secret Edgar G. It's as simple as 1, 2, 3."

"1, 2, 3!" Edgar G repeated. "I don't understand."

Oink explained, "**Look on the ground. Do you see those rocks?**"

Edgar G looked.

"**To move forward, you must count the number of rocks. Then say the number aloud -- all the way through the valley.**"

Edgar shouted, "Y E S! as he leaped up into the air and landed with a bounce very near the edge of the hill.

"WHOA! That was too close.

I've got to remember... *safety*!
Oh! And I've got to remember my numbers.
Oh! And I've got to remember to pray.
Yes! I must pray."

Oink snorted, "Oh Edgar G, you know more than you think you do. If you remember, you just finished counting to three."

"I do remember 1, 2, 3, Edgar said.
But I also know someone who can help me
remember other numbers I learned -- JESUS!
And Holy Spirit will help me
when I pray and ask God my Father in heaven."

Oink said, "Jesus?
Holy Spirit?
God the Father?
Who are they?"

Edgar G answered, *"You don't know who God is?"*

"God made everything in the whole world!

God is the Father.
Jesus is God's Son.
And Holy Spirit is the Spirit of Truth.
These three are one.
(1 John 5:7)

The only true God!"
(John 17:3)

"**Wow!**" said Oink, "**Does God have a Son?**"

Edgar G said, "Yes, He does!
And God loves us all.
My parents told me to *ALWAYS PRAY* and talk to God as my Father. So that's what I am going to do!"

Oink watched as Edgar G closed his eyes.

Edgar prayed:

"Father,
I love you! You always help me.
You help me to choose good things when I pray.
Thank you, Father!
I need your help again.
Will you help me to climb down into this valley safely?
And please help me to remember the numbers I learned.
Thank you, Father!
I know Jesus and Holy Spirit will help me.
Amen"

Edgar G opened his eyes.

Then Oink said,
"I want to know heavenly Father, Jesus and Holy Spirit too.
How do I get to know God?"

Edgar G said, "Just pray and talk to the Father.
Let heavenly Father know that you believe that Jesus is His Son.
When you believe Jesus, heavenly Father, Jesus and Holy Spirit will help you!
But you must remember to pray and ask.
God is a good Father."

Oink said, **"YES, I BELIEVE!"**

Then Oink C Pig closed his eyes and prayed.

He said:

**"Father!
My name is Oink C Pig.
You don't know me, but I want to know you like
Edgar G knows You.
I believe Jesus is your Son.
I understand that You and Jesus made everything.
I really like the things You made.
I want to thank You God that the rock that Edgar G
threw did not hurt me.
I'm going to pray and talk to you more.
Thank You for looking out for me.
Amen"**

After they had both prayed,
Edgar G looked down into the valley.
He stepped back and said,
"Wow, that is a lot of numbers!"

Oink answered, "Oh Edgar G, you don't have to worry. Remember God our Father, Jesus and Holy Spirit will help you to remember. *And* I'm here to help too."

So Edgar G listened as Oink *slowly* counted.
1, 2, 3, 4, 5, 6, 7,

8, 9, 10, and then 11

Oink stopped counting.
He nodded his head with encouragement and looked up at Edgar G.

Before Edgar G hopped, he shouted and thanked God saying,

**"THANK YOU FATHER!
THANK YOU JESUS!
THANK YOU HOLY SPIRIT!**

**Thank You for sending Oink C Pig to help me through this Valley of Numbers!
And I know you are with me."**

Then carefully looking before he leaped,
Edgar G shouted, "1" as he hopped onto his first valley number.

Memory Verses to Teach the Children:

Children, obey your parents the way the LORD wants, because this is the right thing to do.
Ephesians 6:1

Rejoice always. Pray at all times. Give thanks in all circumstances.
1 Thessalonians 5:16-17

Prayer Song to Teach the Children:

(Sung to the tune of the "Up on the Housetop" chorus)
"You can pray, do it today.
You can pray, do it today.
Pray to Father, He's waiting for you.
He will tell you what to do."

Pray and Learn Numbers

Valley of Numbers
Game Instructions

Before beginning the game, carefully cut out the Edgar G Frog game pieces; the game cards; and game sheet located on the next pages, at the back of this book.

1) AT THE BEGINNING OF THE GAME SAY:
God wants us to PRAY AT ALL TIMES!
We can pray and talk to God about anything.
Let's pray before we play.

2) LET EACH CHILD WHO WANTS TO PRAY DO SO.
If no one chooses to pray, an adult (as an example) can say a brief prayer to our heavenly Father and end the prayer by thanking Father. (Remind the children who prayed to thank God after they pray)

TO PLAY VALLEY OF NUMBERS
Number of Players: 2

3) DECIDE WHO WANTS TO PLAY FIRST AND SECOND.
Choose a colored Edgar G. Frog playing piece and place on the game sheet by the feet of Edgar G Frog.
4) MIX THE CARDS
Place the cards in a stack with the frog-side face down within reach of both players.
5) EACH PLAYER, WHEN IT IS THEIR TURN
a. Pull the top card.
b. Hop their playing piece the number of frogs on the card. (Each card has 1, 2, or 3 hops)
c. Name the number on the rock they landed on. IF THE PLAYER DOES NOT KNOW THE NUMBER YET, THEY CAN ASK SOMEONE WHO KNOWS.
6) WHEN A PLAYER LANDS ON THE OINK C. PIG SPACE
The player gets to pull another card and move ahead the number of frogs on the card.
7) WINNING THE GAME
Going through the Valley of Numbers is achieved by pulling a card that would take the player beyond the last number.
8) IF ALL THE CARDS ARE USED AND THE PLAYERS HAVE NOT GONE BEYOND THE LAST NUMBER. Mix the cards and stack them. Then use the cards over again.

Playing Pieces

Cut the playing pieces along the color lines to separate them.
After the four playing pieces are separated, fold the bottom of the playing piece along the white dotted line to stand the piece up on the game sheet.
Extra playing pieces are included.

Option: Use different objects as playing pieces, such as a button and a rock, etc.

Recommended: After cutting to separate the playing pieces, you can keep the game parts, which includes, the playing pieces, cards and game sheet in a zip lock type bag,

 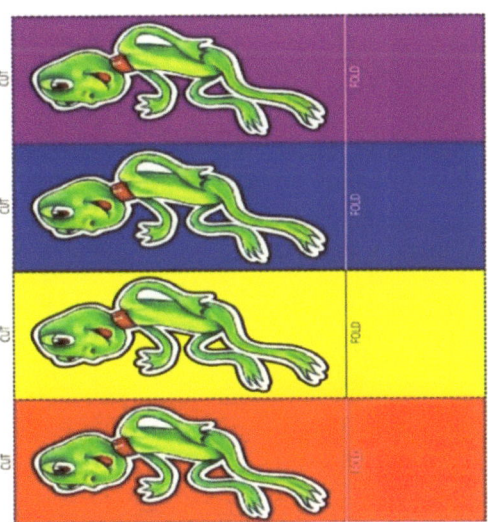

GAME CARDS
Sheet 1 of 2
Cut cards out along the lines

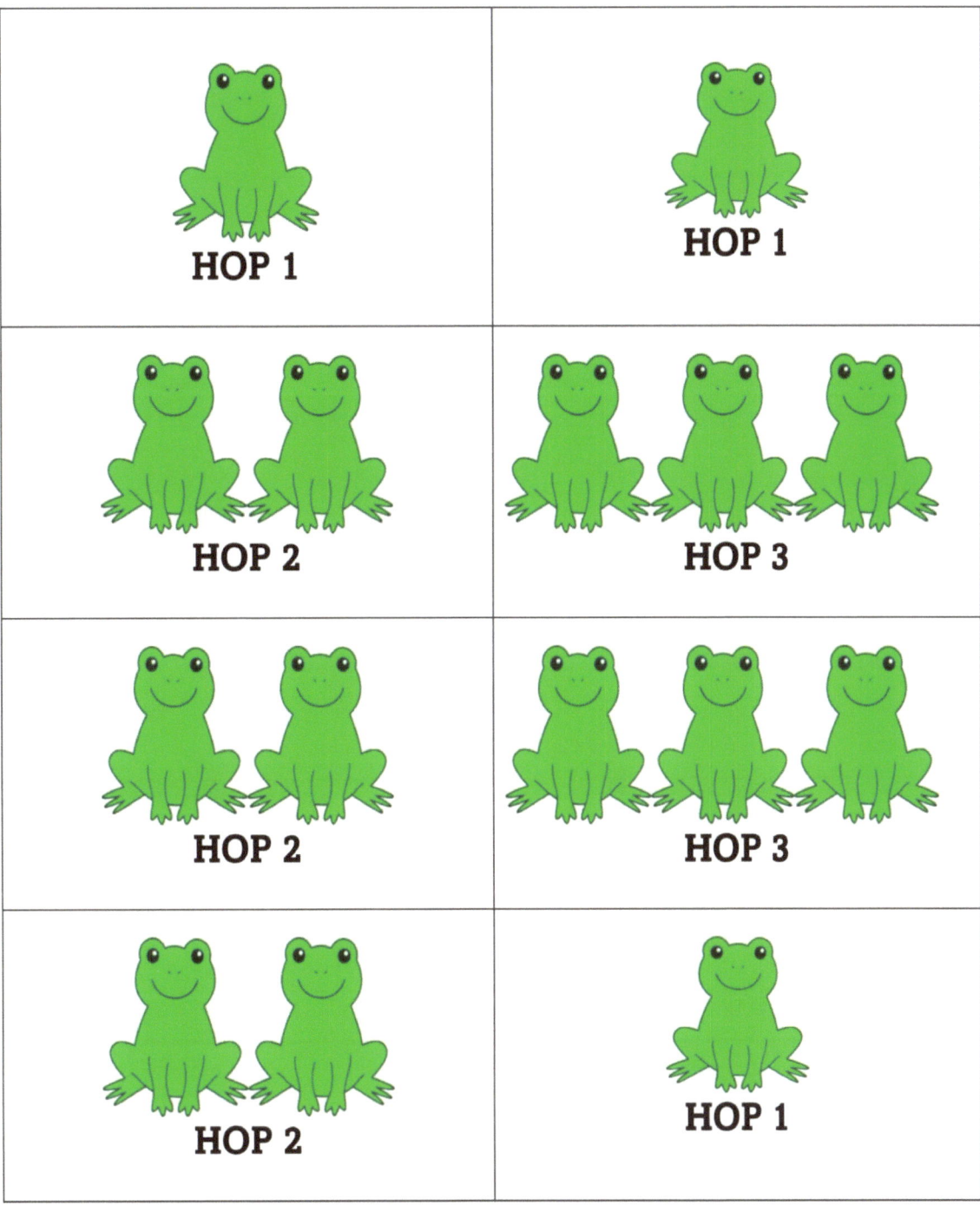

GAME CARDS
Sheet 2 of 2
Cut cards out along the lines

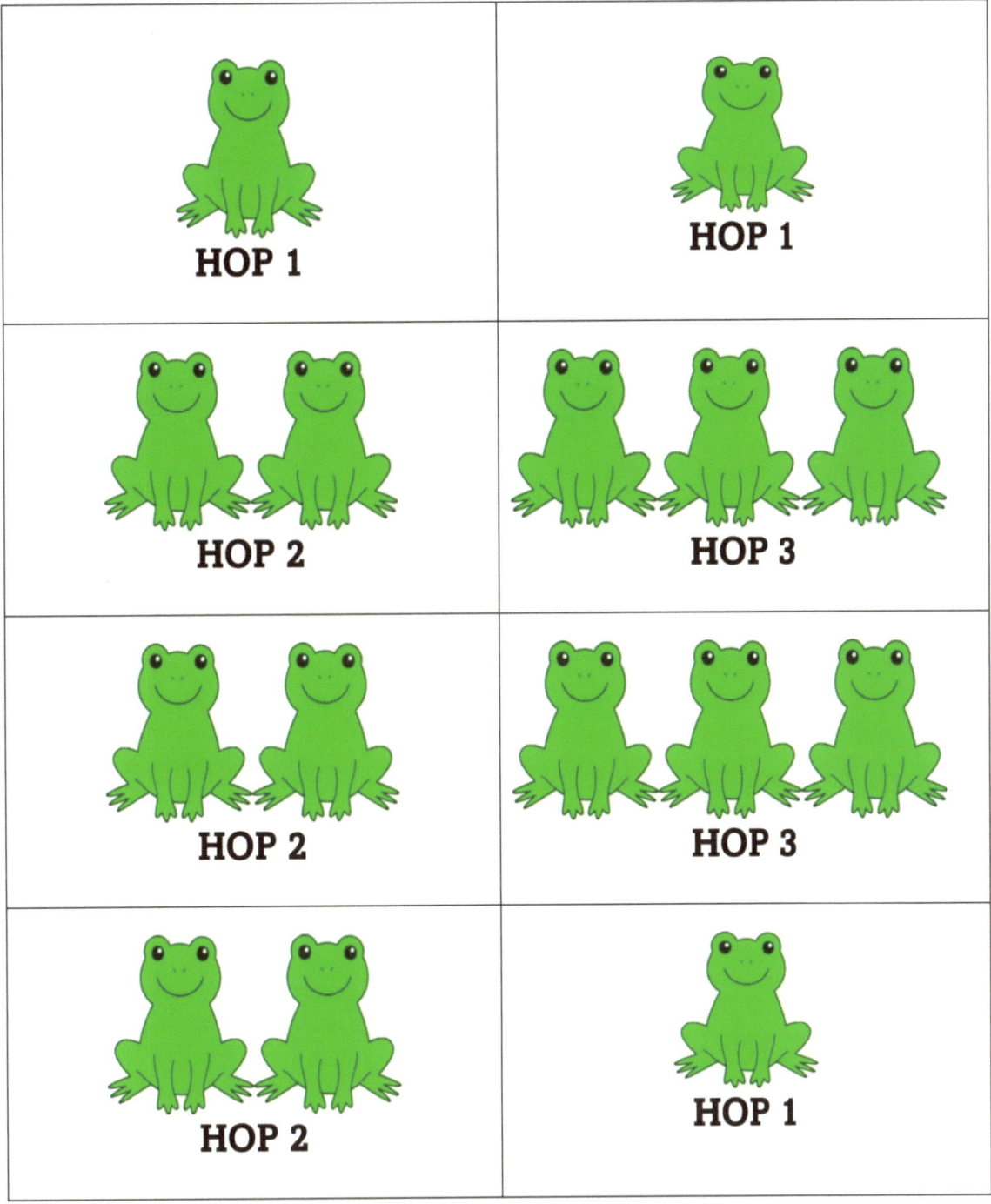

Game Sheet

Cut Here

VALLEY of NUMBERS

Start

1, 2, 3, 4, 5, 6, 7, 8, 9, 10, 11, 12, 13, 14, 15, 16, 17, 18, 19, 20, 1, 2, 3, 4, 5, 6, 7, 8, 9, 10, 11, 12, 13, 14, 15

www.ingramcontent.com/pod-product-compliance
Lightning Source LLC
Chambersburg PA
CBHW041535040426

42446CB00002B/101